PRO SPORTS
BIOGRAPHIES

CAM NEWTON

by Elizabeth Raum

D1408825

AMICUS HIGH INTEREST • AMICUS INK

Amicus High Interest and Amicus Ink are imprints of Amicus
P.O. Box 1329, Mankato, MN 56002
www.amicuspublishing.us

Library of Congress Cataloging-in-Publication Data
Names: Raum, Elizabeth, author.
Title: Cam Newton / by Elizabeth Raum.
Description: Mankato, MN : Amicus High Interest/Amicus Ink, 2018. |
 Series: Amicus High Interest. Pro Sports Biographies | Includes index. |
 Audience: K to 3.
Identifiers: LCCN 2017003892 (print) | LCCN 2017004111 (ebook) | ISBN
 9781681511375 (library bound) | ISBN 9781681521688 (pbk.) | ISBN
 9781681512273 (ebook)
Subjects: LCSH: Newton, Cam, 1989---Juvenile literature. | Football
 players--United States--Biography--Juvenile literature. | Quarterbacks
 (Football)--United States--Biography.
Classification: LCC GV939.N42 R38 2018 (print) | LCC GV939.N42 (ebook) |
 DDC 796.332092 [B] --dc23
LC record available at https://lccn.loc.gov/2017003892

Photo Credits: Erik S. Lesser/epa
european pressphoto agency b.v./Alamy
Stock Photo cover; AP Photo/Tom DiPace 4–5;
Sam Greenwood/Getty Images 7; Dave Martin/AP/REX/
Shutterstock 8–9, 22; Kelly Kline/REUTERS/Alamy Stock Photo
11; AP Photo/Paul Abell 12–13; AP Photo/Charlie Riedel 2, 14–15;
AP Photo/Tony Avelar 16–17; Tinseltown/Shutterstock, Inc. 19;
Emma McIntyre Getty Images 20–21

Editor: Wendy Dieker
Designer: Aubrey Harper
Photo Researcher: Holly Young

Printed in the United States of America

HC 10 9 8 7 6 5 4 3 2 1
PB 10 9 8 7 6 5 4 3 2 1

TABLE OF CONTENTS

SUPERCAM

Touchdown! Cam Newton scores again. He pretends to pull open his shirt like Superman. Newton is the **quarterback** (QB) for the Carolina Panthers. His fans call him SuperCam.

STARTING OUT

Cam Newton grew up in Georgia. In high school, he was a football star. He wanted to play college football. Newton went to the University of Florida in 2007. He joined the football team.

A NEW START

In 2008, Newton hurt his ankle. He couldn't play ball. He left the team. In 2010, Newton got a new start. He moved to Auburn in Alabama to play football.

A GOOD LEADER

Newton was a good leader at Auburn. The team won the **NCAA** championship game. Newton won the Heisman Trophy that year. This award goes to the best player in college football.

GOING PRO

In 2011, Newton went **pro**. The Carolina Panthers picked him. The Panthers were the worst team that year. They hoped that Newton would help them win.

SUPER BOWL

Newton did help the Panthers. They started winning more games. In 2015, they won 15 games. They lost only one. Newton led them to the **Super Bowl**. They lost to the Denver Broncos.

Newton was named the 2015 NFL Most Valuable Player (MVP).

SETTING A RECORD

In 2016, Newton set an NFL record. From 2011 to 2016, he made 48 **rushing touchdowns**. That was the most ever by a QB. Not many QBs carry the ball into the end zone. But Newton does.

STYLE ICON

Off the field, Newton likes to wear flashy clothes. He wears fancy hats. His shoes are always stylish. No one else dresses like Newton.

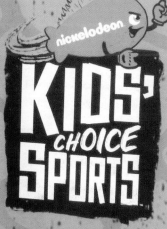

KID AT HEART

People say Newton is a kid at heart. Newton hosts a TV show called *All In with Cam Newton*. He tells kids to dream big. He wants their dreams to come true. His did.

Newton spent a day with young football players. They filmed a TV ad.

JUST THE FACTS

Born: May 11, 1989

Hometown: Atlanta, Georgia

Colleges: University of Florida (2007–2008); Blinn College (2009); Auburn University (2010–2011)

Joined the pros: 2011

Position: Quarterback

Stats: www.nfl.com/player/camnewton/2495455/careerstats

Accomplishments:

- Heisman Trophy winner: 2010

- NFL AP Offensive Rookie of the Year: 2011

- Pro Bowl appearances: 2011, 2013, 2015

- Super Bowl appearances: 2016

- NFL Most Valuable Player: 2015

- Set record for most rushing TDs by a QB: 2016 (48 career TDs)

WORDS TO KNOW

NCAA (National Collegiate Athletic Association) – the organization that makes rules for college football games

NFL (National Football League) – the organization that makes the rules for the professional American football league

pro – short for professional; a person who is paid to play sports

quarterback – the player who leads the offense by throwing the ball or handing it to a runner

rushing touchdown – a touchdown earned by a player running the ball into the end zone, rather than by catching a pass

Super Bowl – the game at the end of the NFL football season between the best two NFL teams that year

LEARN MORE

Books

Doeden, Matt. *Football's Greatest Quarterbacks*. North Mankato, Minn.: Capstone, 2015.

Fishman, Jon M. *Cam Newton*. Minneapolis: Lerner, 2017.

Kelley, K. C. *Football Superstars 2016*. New York: Scholastic, 2016.

Websites

The Cam Newton Foundation
https://www.cam1newton.com/

The Official Site of the Carolina Panthers
http://www.panthers.com/

INDEX